LIVING WITH MOM, LIVING WITH DAD

BY HOLLY DUHIG

KidHaven
PUBLISHING

Published in 2019 by KidHaven Publishing, an Imprint of Greenhaven Publishing, LLC
353 3rd Avenue, Suite 255, New York, NY 10010

© 2019 Booklife Publishing

This edition is published by arrangement with Booklife Publishing.

Written by: Holly Duhig
Edited by: Kirsty Holmes
Designed by: Danielle Rippengill

Cataloging-in-Publication Data

Names: Duhig, Holly.
Title: Living with mom, living with dad / Holly Duhig.
Description: New York : KidHaven Publishing, 2019. | Series: Topics to talk about | Includes glossary and index.
Identifiers: ISBN 9781534526525 (pbk.) | ISBN 9781534526518 (library bound) | ISBN 9781534526532 (6 pack)
Subjects: LCSH: Children of divorced parents--Juvenile literature. | Divorce--Juvenile literature.
Classification: LCC HQ777.5 D84 2019 | DDC 306.89--dc23

Image Credits: All images are courtesy of Shutterstock.com, unless otherwise specified. With thanks to Getty Images, Thinkstock Photo and iStockphoto.
Front Cover – wavebreakmedia, prapann, Alexander Lysenko, Mc Satori, Ian 2010, xpixel, Max Lashcheuski, pingebat, . Images used on every spread
– Red_Spruce, MG Drachal, Alexander Lysenko, Kues, Flas100, Kanate, Nikolaeva. 1 – wavebreakmedia, prapann. 2 & 4 – wavebreakmedia. 5 – Ewelina
Wachala, 1000 Words. 6 – Malykalexa. 7–11 wavebreakmedia. 12 – kurhan. 13 – wavebreakmedia. 14 & 15 – Africa Studio. 16 – iordani. 16 & 17
– Photographee.eu. 18– 20 – wavebreakmedia. 21 – Cineberg. 22 & 23 – wavebreakmedia.

Printed in the United States of America

CPSIA compliance information: Batch # BS18KL: For further information contact Greenhaven Publishing LLC, New York, New York at 1-844-317-7404.

CONTENTS

WORDS THAT LOOK LIKE **THIS** CAN BE FOUND IN THE GLOSSARY ON PAGE 24.

MY FAMILY

My name is Anna, and this is my family. Here I am with
my little brother, Luca, and our parents, Gael and Julia.

Although we are a family, we don't live all together anymore. A while ago, Mom and Dad decided to divorce, so now they live in different houses.

MOM'S HOUSE

DAD'S HOUSE

LIVING APART

Divorce is when two people who were married decide they don't want to be married anymore.

PEOPLE SOMETIMES GO TO COURT TO GET DIVORCED.

Divorce can be sad at first, but it is sometimes for the best. Mom and Dad used to argue a lot. After a while, they realized they would be happier if they lived apart.

My parents said they were separating because they were not in love with each other anymore. They both still love me and Luca very much, though.

I didn't want Mom and Dad to divorce at first. I asked if they would ever get remarried again. Mom said they wouldn't, and that separating was for the best.

Feeling Sad 🙁

When Mom first told me and Luca that Dad was going to move out, I felt really sad and cried a lot. I was worried that Dad wanted to move out because of something I had done.

DIVORCE IS NEVER YOUR FAULT.

I asked Dad if I wasn't being well-behaved enough. Dad told me that moving out was his decision and it would never be my fault, no matter how I behaved.

⭐ ⭐

My Homes

We all helped Dad move in.

Luca and I have two homes now. This is because Mom lives in our old house and Dad moved to a new house. Both of our homes are _unique_.

While Dad moved into his house, Luca and I lived with Mom. Now we live at Mom's one week and at Dad's the week after.

MOM AND DAD HAVE JOINT CUSTODY OF ME AND LUCA.

My best friend Callum goes to my **gymnastics** class. His parents are divorced, too. He used to live with his mom, but now he only lives with his dad.

CALLUM'S PARENTS HAVE BEEN DIVORCED FOR A WHILE.

CALLUM AND HIS DAD

Callum told me that moving to a new house feels like moving to a new school. You might feel worried at first, but it soon feels normal.

My Bedrooms

My bedroom at Dad's house is very pretty. I try to keep it tidy.

It gets a bit messy when Luca and I play in it, though!

My bedroom at Mom's house is pink, too, and has a desk. This is where I do my homework.

AT LEAST I ALWAYS HAVE LUCA WITH ME!

Sometimes I miss Mom when I'm staying at Dad's house, and I miss Dad when I'm staying at Mom's house.

I used to worry that my parents would be upset if I told them I missed my other house, but they both understood.

DAD HELPS ME TALK TO MOM WHEN I'M AT HIS HOUSE.

New Beginnings

During the school break, Dad **introduced** me to his new girlfriend, Sarah. I felt really shy at first, and I didn't want to speak to Sarah. I wanted to keep my dad all to myself.

After a while, though, I started speaking to Sarah more and more. She is a police officer, so she has lots of cool stories.

I WANT TO BE A POLICE OFFICER ONE DAY, TOO!

As time goes by, families grow and change. This can be a good thing. Mom and Dad are happier now than ever before.

AND AS FOR ME AND LUCA, WE EACH HAVE TWO BEDROOMS WITH TWO SETS OF TOYS AND GAMES!

Some families live together and some don't. But one thing's for sure – all families love each other very much.

Glossary and Index

Glossary

court	a place where legal decisions can be made
gymnastics	a type of exercise that improves strength and balance
introduced	made someone known to another person
joint custody	an arrangement where parents who are divorced both look after a child and both give the child a home for some of the time
separating	deciding to live apart from a partner
unique	being the only one of its kind

Index